T0142518

# Alphabet
# of
# FLOWERS

## GLORIA D. GONSALVES

AuthorHouse™ UK
1663 Liberty Drive
Bloomington, IN 47403  USA
www.authorhouse.co.uk
UK TFN: 0800 0148641 (Toll Free inside the UK)
UK Local: 02036 956322 (+44 20 3695 6322 from outside the UK)

Because of the dynamic nature of the Internet, any web addresses or links contained in this book may have changed since publication and may no longer be valid. The views expressed in this work are solely those of the author and do not necessarily reflect the views of the publisher, and the publisher hereby disclaims any responsibility for them.

This book is printed on acid-free paper.

ISBN: 978-1-6655-9726-5 (sc)
ISBN: 978-1-6655-9735-7 (hc)
ISBN: 978-1-6655-9727-2 (e)

Print information available on the last page.

Published by AuthorHouse  03/15/2022

**author**HOUSE®

# AUNTIE GLO'S

# ALPHABET OF FLOWERS

**A** is for Amaranth.

Amaranth flowers are red or green.

They keep their colour even when dry.

People grow them as decoration or eat the leaves as vegetable.

**B** is for Bougainvillea.

Bougainvillea actual flowers are small and white.

The colourful part is called a bract and inside are the flowers.

People grow them in the garden or to decorate fences.

**C** is for Calla Lily.

Calla lilies are originally from South Africa.

They are popular at weddings.

Next time you're at a wedding, see if you can find the calla lily.

# D is for Daisy.

Daisies are wildflowers.

They are eaten in salads or used to decorate cakes.

Did you know you can wear them in your hair? Try making a daisy chain when you see a big patch of them.

# E is for Echinacea.

Echinacea's common name is coneflower.

The centre of the flower looks like a cone.

People use it in cough medicine.

# F

is for Frangipani.

Frangipani is a tropical flower.

It is used in soaps and massage oils.

Did you know you can make a garland to wear around your neck? The flower looks pretty in hair too.

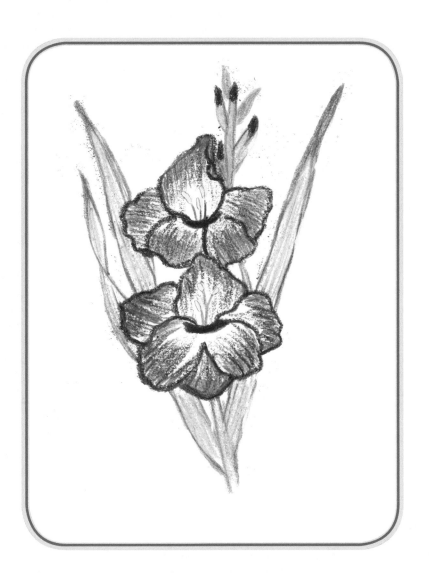

**G** is for Gladiolus.

Gladiolus is also known as sword lily.

This tall flower can win your heart like a gladiator.

The original plant grows wild in South Africa.

**H** is for Hibiscus.

The hibiscus flower has five petals.

The flowers are large and colourful.

Have you tried hibiscus tea?

I is for Iris.

The iris has two parts with upward and downward petals.

They are showy flowers.

Some people name their children Iris.

**J** is for Jasmine.

Jasmine flowers are white.

The flowers open up at night.

Their floral smell is stronger at night than during the day.

**K** is for Kniphofia.

Kniphofias have the warm colours of fire.

The flowers droop down like a torch.

Their common name is torch lilies or red hot poker.

**L** is for Lavender.

Lavender flowers are purple.

Their smell is like perfume.

It is used in food such as ice cream.

**M** is for Morning Glory.

The morning glory flowers bloom in the morning.

They are funnel-shaped.

Their leaves shape will remind you of love.

**N** is for Narcissus.

An example of a narcissus flower is the daffodil.

Daffodils grow from a bulb that looks like an onion.

The trumpet part is called the corona.

**O** is for Okra.

The okra flower looks like a hibiscus.

It blooms only for a day, then falls off.

The flowers can be eaten raw or cooked.

**P** is for Poppy.

The common poppy has a red colour.

Some poppies are grown for eating.

Edible seeds are used as toppings for bread and cookies.

**Q** is for Queen's Cup.

The queen's cup flower is white.

It has a shape like a star.

They grow on the forest floor.

# R is for Rose.

A rose has a beautiful smell like perfume.

It has thorns to help it climb.

Rose petals are used in making confetti for parties.

**S** is for Sunflower.

A sunflower looks like the sun.

Young sunflowers turn to follow the sun.

Sunflower oil is made from flower seeds.

**T** is for Tulip.

Tulips have different colours including yellow, orange, red, purple, pink and white.

The largest tulip garden is in The Netherlands.

People connect tulips with the spring season.

**U** is for Ursinia.

An ursinia is an African daisy.

It is a bright yellow-orange colour.

The flower reminds you of the sun.

# V is for Violet.

Violets can grow wild in the forest.

African violets are only found in East Africa.

They are popular houseplants.

**W** is for Waterlily.

Waterlilies grow in water.

The beautiful flowers float above the water.

They have a cup shape.

 is for Xanthisma.

The xanthisma flower looks like a yellow daisy.

It is also known as a sleepy-daisy.

The flower sleeps at night and opens up during the day.

**Y** is for Yellow Oleander.

The yellow oleander is yellow or orange.

It is a beautiful tropical flower.

Be careful because it is poisonous.

**Z** is for Zinnia.

Zinnias are many colours like the rainbow.

The colours have different meanings for people.

For example, pink ones are gifted to family and friends.

# THE END

# SUMMARY TABLE

| | |
|---|---|
| **A**maranth | 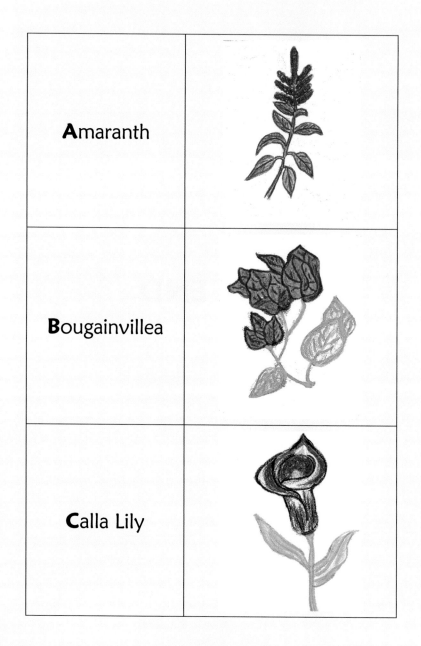 |
| **B**ougainvillea | |
| **C**alla Lily | |

**D**aisy

**E**chinacea

**F**rangipani

| **G**ladiolus | 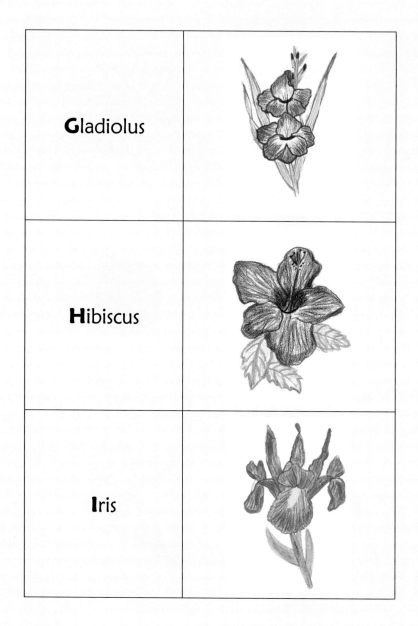 |
| **H**ibiscus | |
| **I**ris | |

| | |
|---|---|
| **J**asmine |  |
| **K**niphofia | |
| **L**avender | |

| | |
|---|---|
| **M**orning Glory |  |
| **N**arcissus | |
| **O**kra | |

| | |
|---|---|
| **P**oppy |  |
| **Q**ueen's Cup | |
| **R**ose | |

| | |
|---|---|
| **S**unflower | 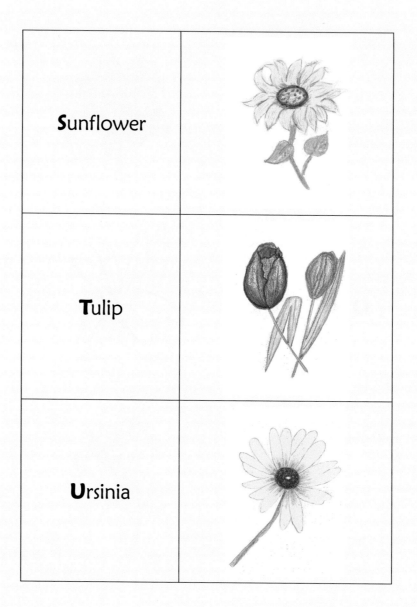 |
| **T**ulip | |
| **U**rsinia | |

**V**iolet

**W**aterlily

**X**anthisma

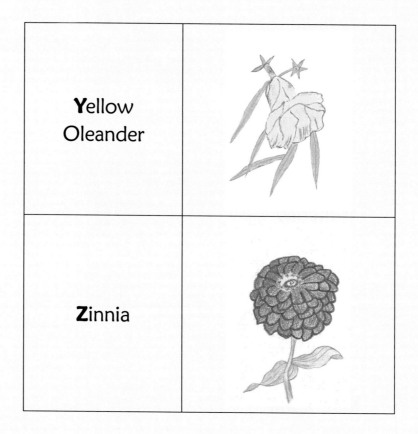

**Y**ellow
Oleander

**Z**innia

# COMPLETE THE FOLLOWING FLOWER ALPHABETS

Aa _____     Nn _____

Bb _____     Oo _____

Cc _____     Pp _____

Dd _____     Qq _____

Ee _____     Rr _____

Ff _____     Ss _____

Gg _____     Tt _____

Hh _____     Uu _____

Ii _____     Vv _____

Jj _____     Ww _____

Kk _____     Xx _____

Ll _____     Yy _____

Mm _____     Zz _____

# EXPLORE, DRAW AND PAINT A FLOWER

Printed in the United States
by Baker & Taylor Publisher Services